Copyright © 2016 Jane E

All rights reserved.
First Printing, 2016
ISBN 978-0-9981899-5-6

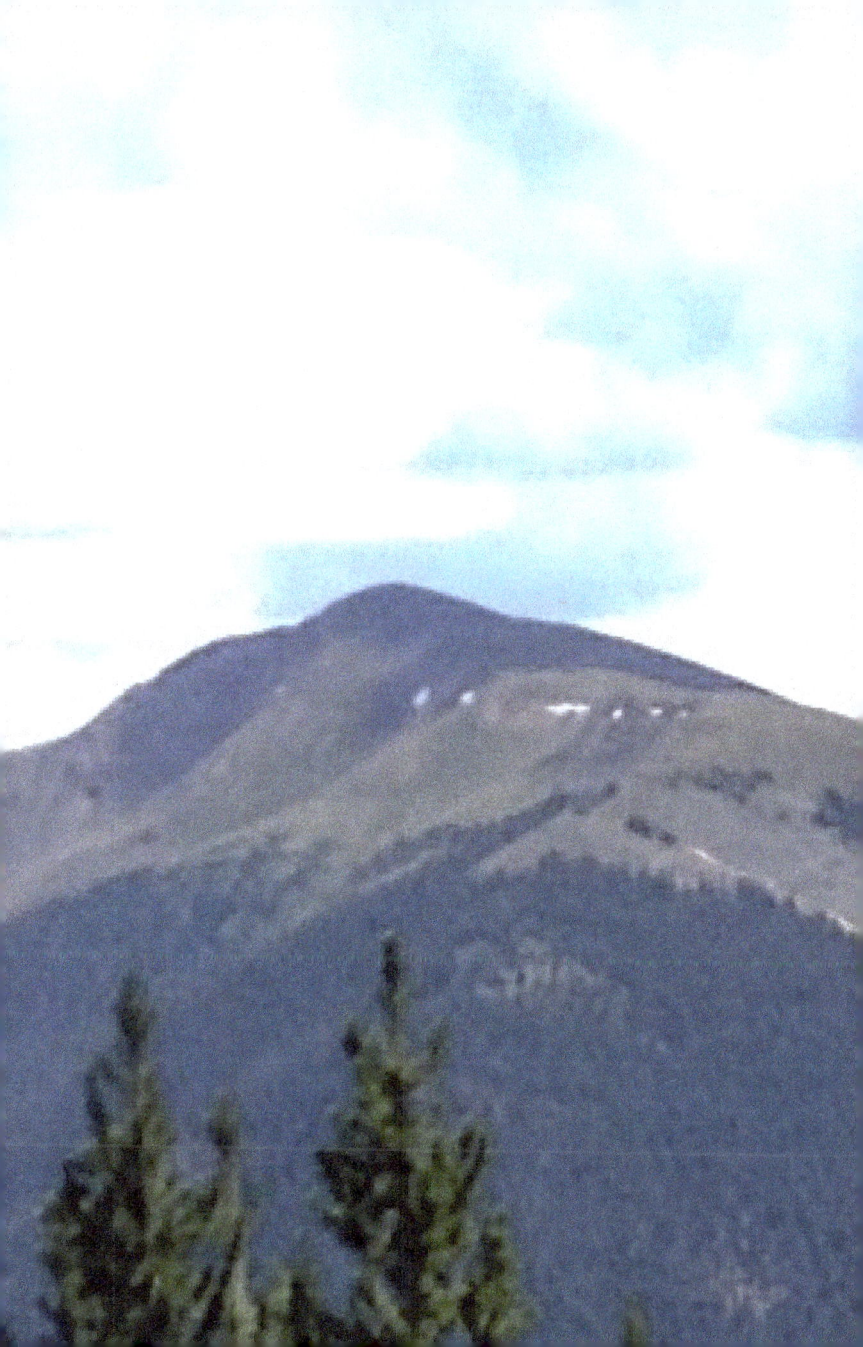

Foreword

Laura and her mother, Jane, are a unique union of exceptional intellect and intense spiritual growth. Enjoying a loving relationship that is a model for mothers and daughters everywhere, they are a perfect compliment to each other. For nearly four decades, Jane has inspired hundreds of women and men who seek to defend their minds and souls from the attack of addictive substances. Laura too chooses to abstain from these deadly soul-destroying threats.

I urge you to read this volume slowly and reverently. Let this experience seep into your heart and, I'm sure, you too will be transformed.

Gene M

Introduction

Hi...I am Jane and I am an alcoholic. And I am a grateful recovering alcoholic. I think that from the moment of my conception, my genetic composition somehow predetermined my life direction. My personality traits indicate sensitivity, obsessive-compulsiveness, intelligence, defiance/stubbornness, impatience, appreciation of nature, and naiveness.

Several weeks after the first sharing of this story, I played golf with friends and subsequently sat in the club room sharing conversation and watching the 2016 Ryder Cup being played at Hazeltine National Golf Club in Minneapolis. My friends each enjoyed a pleasant hour sharing stories while drinking a couple of beers. I drank my water and noticed my unusual quietness. Even with 40+ years of sobriety, a part of my brain questioned my addiction and suggested that perhaps a little alcohol would liven me up.

The thought stayed with me for the next hour UNTIL I remembered all that I had written the previous summer - and all that my daughter had shared - the suffering and relationship destructions that my disease caused. The next morning I shared this event with a sponsor and reiterated the passion I have for our twelve-step way of life. I know myself well enough to realize that the most effective way to inflict self-punishment would be to imbibe a chemical substance.

Finding Our Way describes the descent into self destruction of body, soul, mind that chemical addiction causes and how this is a family disease. The only solution to this fatal problem is to become aware of absolute personal powerlessness and the subsequent dependence upon a Higher Power to remove the obsession to rely on chemicals in order to overcome the travails on life's odyssey.

Part One
Jane

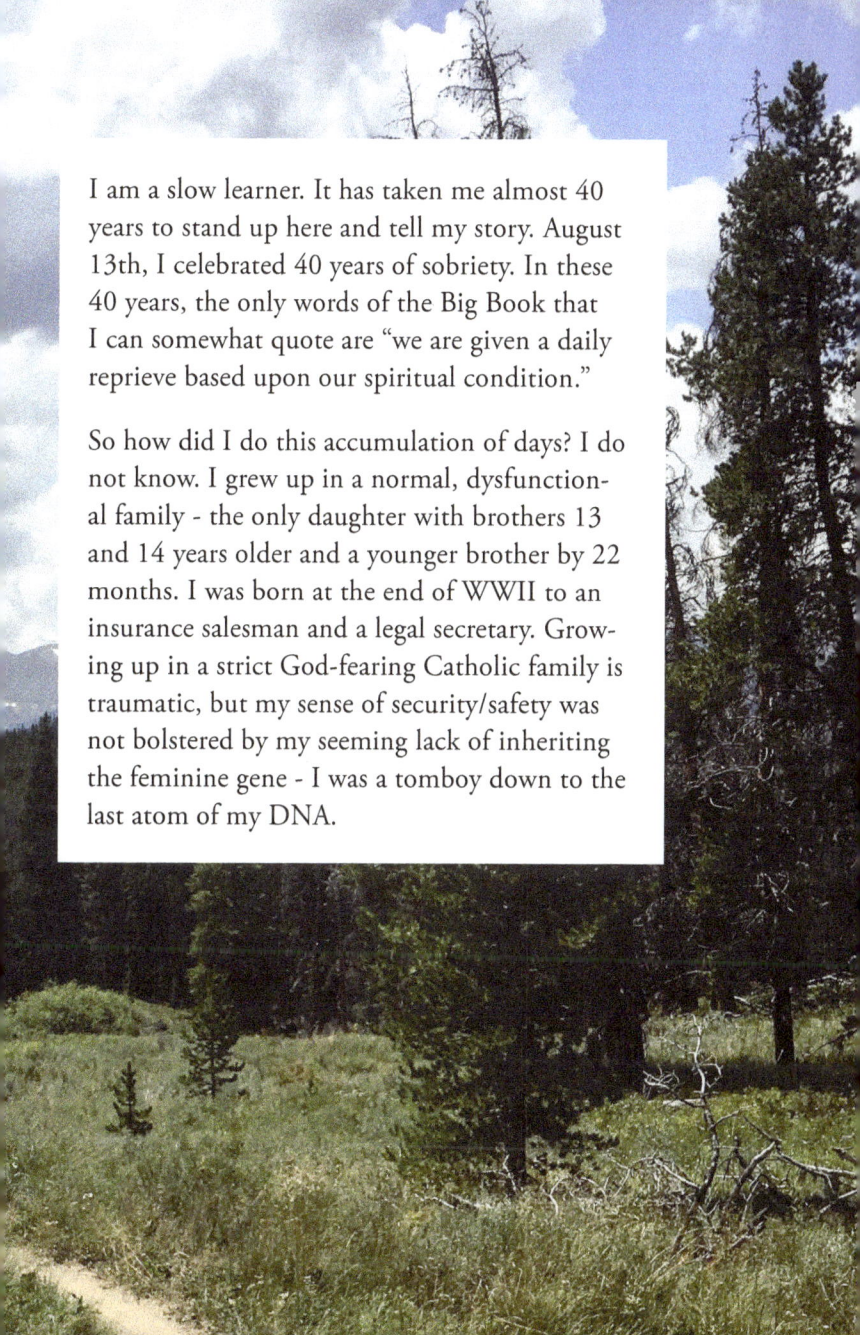

I am a slow learner. It has taken me almost 40 years to stand up here and tell my story. August 13th, I celebrated 40 years of sobriety. In these 40 years, the only words of the Big Book that I can somewhat quote are "we are given a daily reprieve based upon our spiritual condition."

So how did I do this accumulation of days? I do not know. I grew up in a normal, dysfunctional family - the only daughter with brothers 13 and 14 years older and a younger brother by 22 months. I was born at the end of WWII to an insurance salesman and a legal secretary. Growing up in a strict God-fearing Catholic family is traumatic, but my sense of security/safety was not bolstered by my seeming lack of inheriting the feminine gene - I was a tomboy down to the last atom of my DNA.

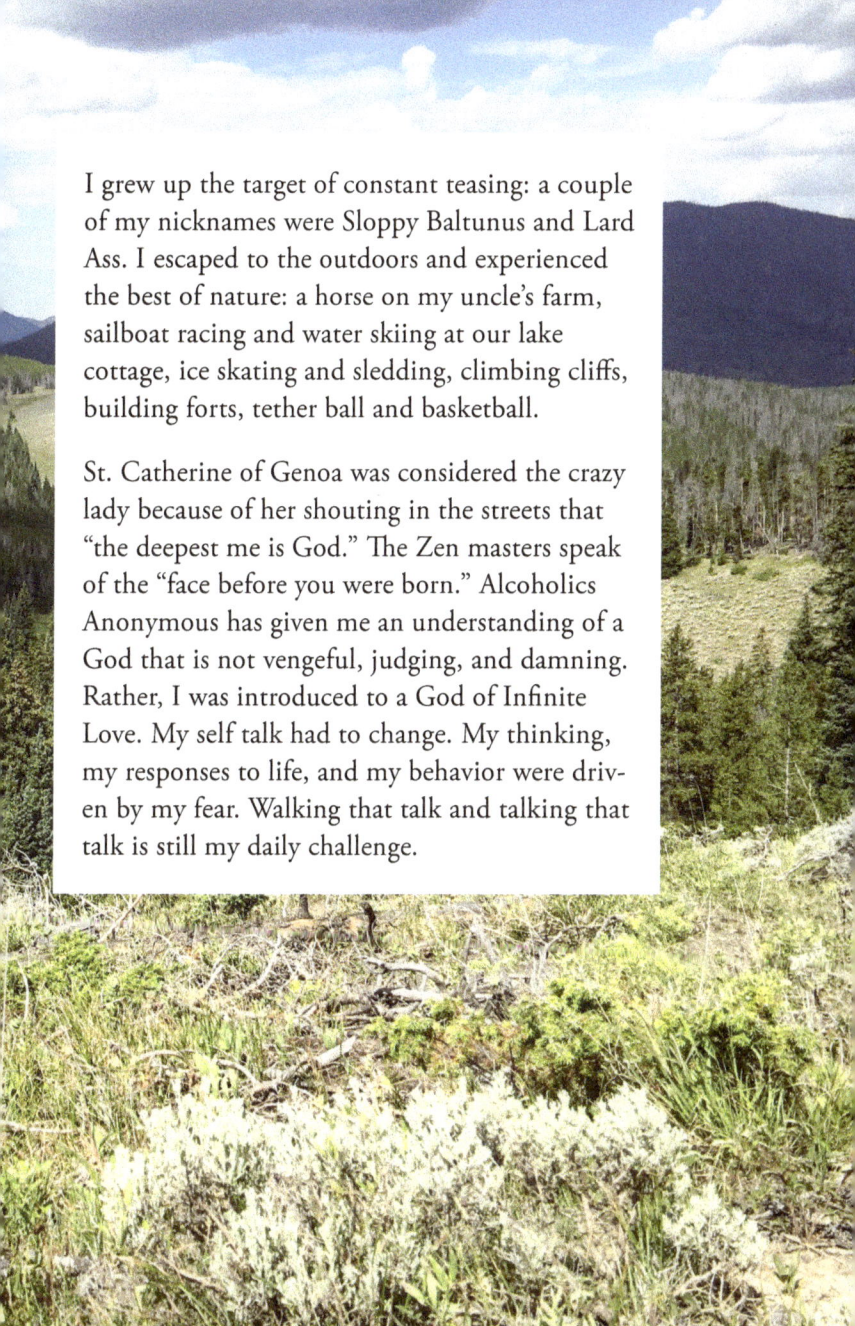

I grew up the target of constant teasing: a couple of my nicknames were Sloppy Baltunus and Lard Ass. I escaped to the outdoors and experienced the best of nature: a horse on my uncle's farm, sailboat racing and water skiing at our lake cottage, ice skating and sledding, climbing cliffs, building forts, tether ball and basketball.

St. Catherine of Genoa was considered the crazy lady because of her shouting in the streets that "the deepest me is God." The Zen masters speak of the "face before you were born." Alcoholics Anonymous has given me an understanding of a God that is not vengeful, judging, and damning. Rather, I was introduced to a God of Infinite Love. My self talk had to change. My thinking, my responses to life, and my behavior were driven by my fear. Walking that talk and talking that talk is still my daily challenge.

I married at age 22. My younger brother told me during my senior college year Christmas break that I had better date this guy because no one else could ever be interested in me, and my history with boys was proving that data. A year and half later I whispered to my dad as we walked down the church aisle towards the five priests concelebrating our wedding Mass that I really did not want to do this. Dad gripped my arm tighter and said it was too late to change my mind.

Up to this point, my drinking did not seem problematic. I graduated with a degree in science teaching and I taught a year in Richfield. I was miserable and incredibly lonely and frightened and becoming more aware of my fiancé's drinking. I kept a bottle of wine in the refrigerator and discovered that a couple of glasses of wine each evening numbed my jitters.

I had started having panic attacks when I was 16, thus aggravating my self loathing and self pity. Marriage was not the solution to my fears and only triggered a fast track to alcoholism. My husband was 7 years older, a music teacher, and reared in an apartment over his parent's bar in a small town. We fought and drank daily. If it were a choice of buying food for supper or a bottle of cheap wine, the Gallo wine was purchased. My beautiful daughter was born 14 months into the marriage and her sister came along 5 years later. We hooked up with a group of heavy drinkers. I thought I had my life under control: a substitute teaching job, a new home, sailboat racing in a prestigious yacht club, a golfing membership at the country club, two beautiful daughters, and doing Catholicism to the letter of the law. But my pain was so intense and self referential I thought I was losing my mind when

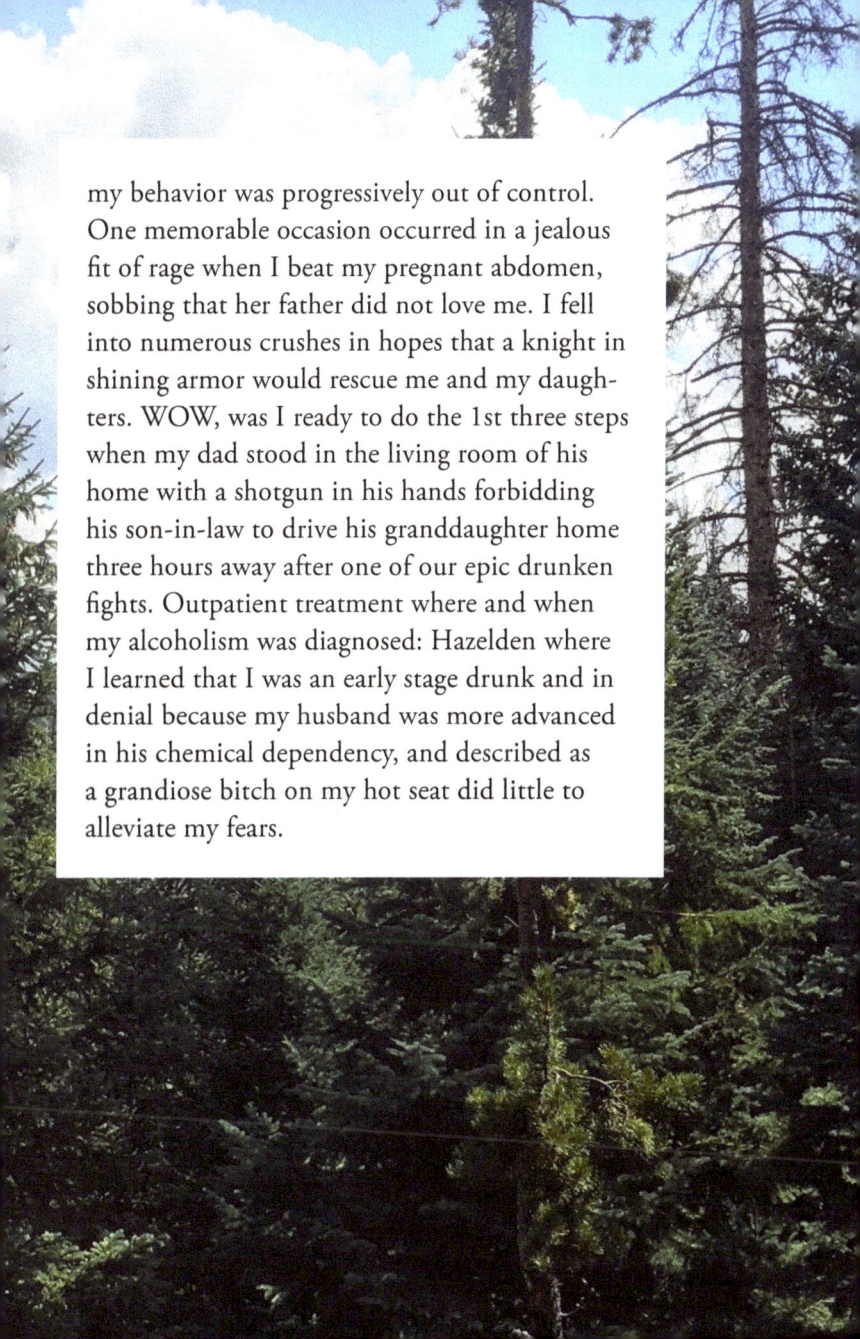

my behavior was progressively out of control. One memorable occasion occurred in a jealous fit of rage when I beat my pregnant abdomen, sobbing that her father did not love me. I fell into numerous crushes in hopes that a knight in shining armor would rescue me and my daughters. WOW, was I ready to do the 1st three steps when my dad stood in the living room of his home with a shotgun in his hands forbidding his son-in-law to drive his granddaughter home three hours away after one of our epic drunken fights. Outpatient treatment where and when my alcoholism was diagnosed: Hazelden where I learned that I was an early stage drunk and in denial because my husband was more advanced in his chemical dependency, and described as a grandiose bitch on my hot seat did little to alleviate my fears.

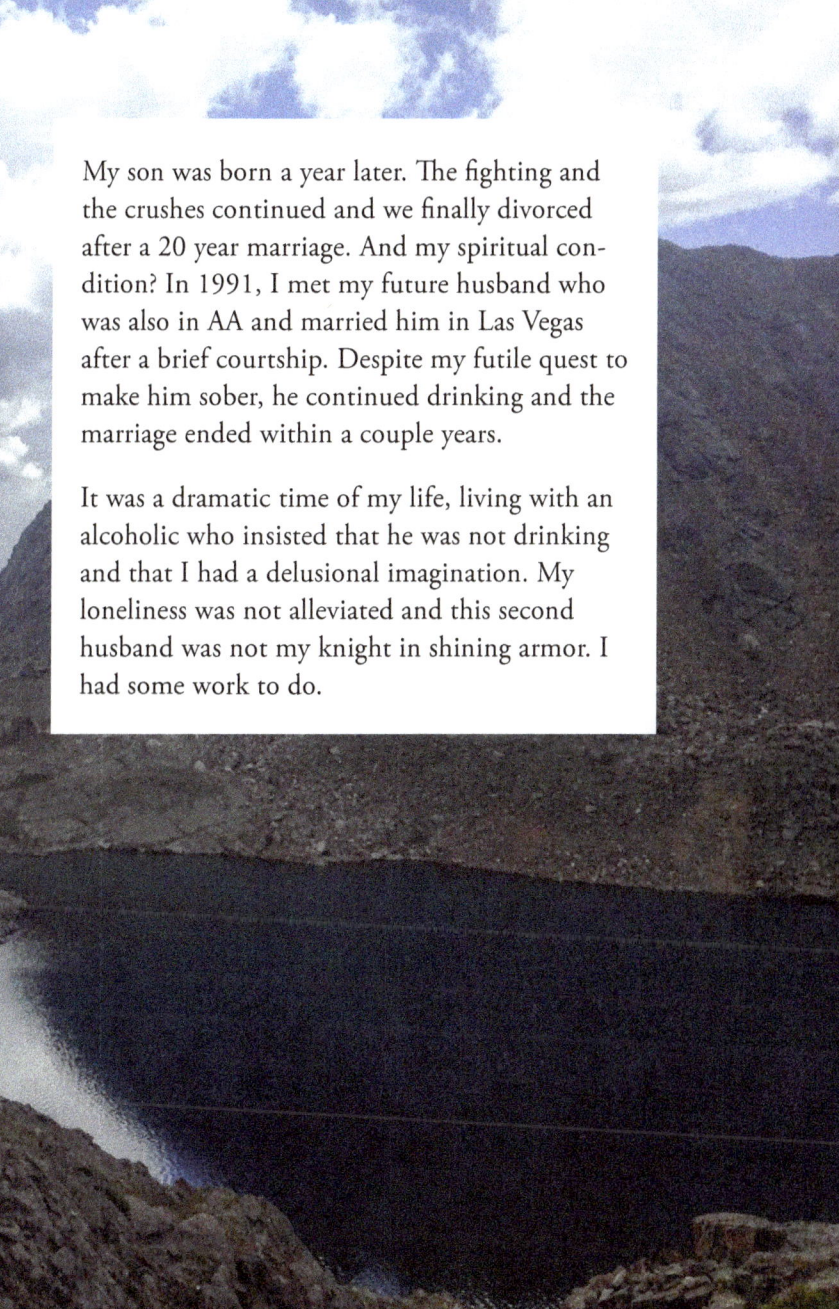

My son was born a year later. The fighting and the crushes continued and we finally divorced after a 20 year marriage. And my spiritual condition? In 1991, I met my future husband who was also in AA and married him in Las Vegas after a brief courtship. Despite my futile quest to make him sober, he continued drinking and the marriage ended within a couple years.

It was a dramatic time of my life, living with an alcoholic who insisted that he was not drinking and that I had a delusional imagination. My loneliness was not alleviated and this second husband was not my knight in shining armor. I had some work to do.

Part One
Laura

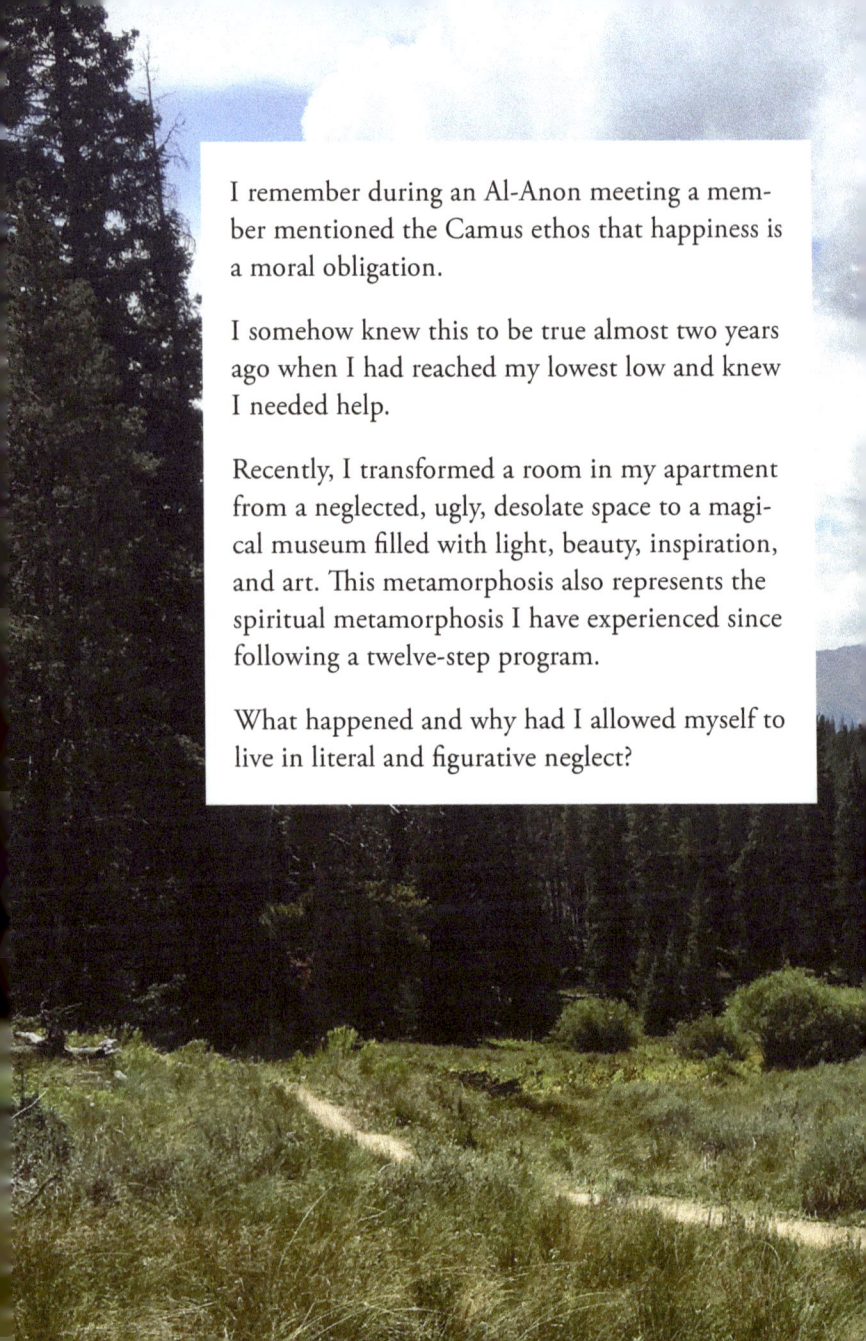

I remember during an Al-Anon meeting a member mentioned the Camus ethos that happiness is a moral obligation.

I somehow knew this to be true almost two years ago when I had reached my lowest low and knew I needed help.

Recently, I transformed a room in my apartment from a neglected, ugly, desolate space to a magical museum filled with light, beauty, inspiration, and art. This metamorphosis also represents the spiritual metamorphosis I have experienced since following a twelve-step program.

What happened and why had I allowed myself to live in literal and figurative neglect?

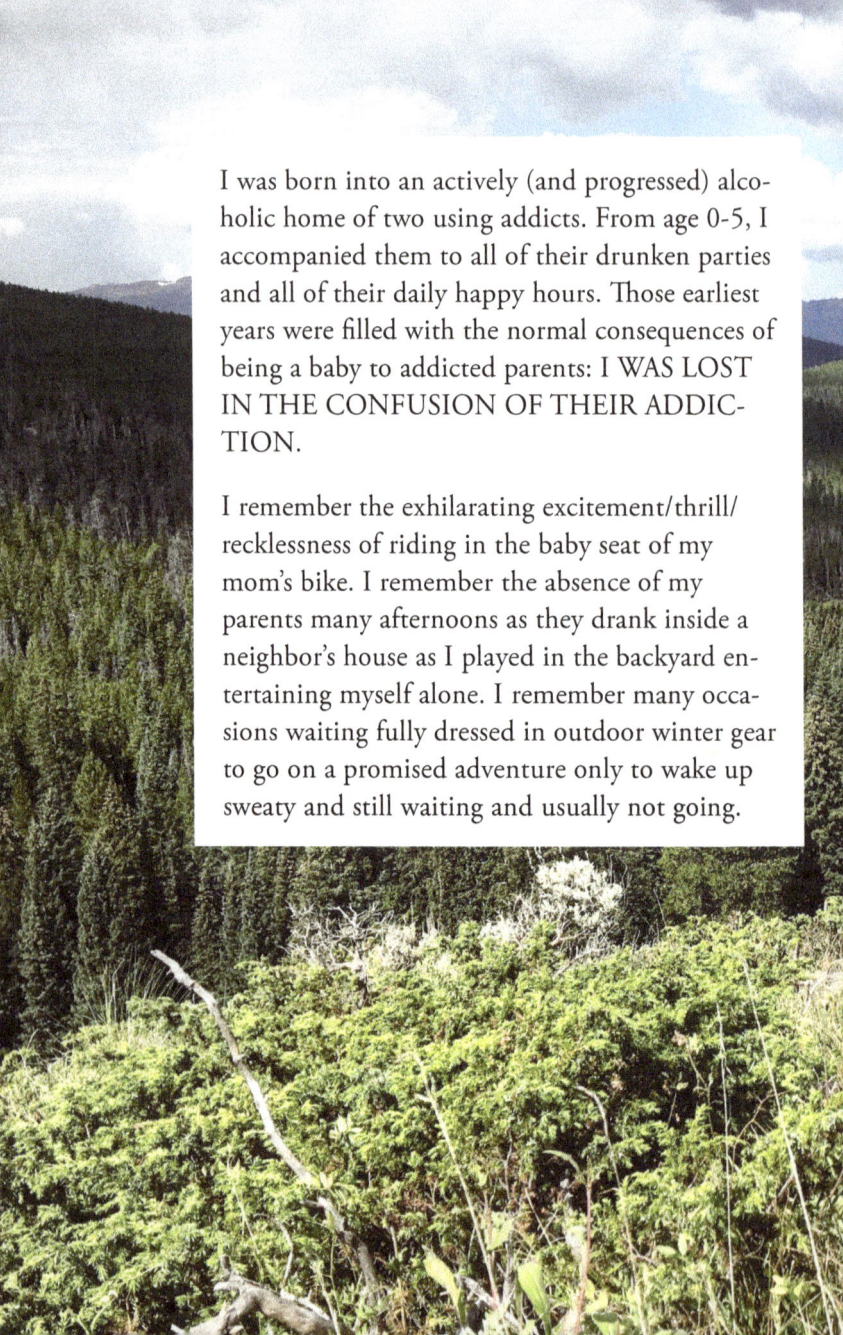

I was born into an actively (and progressed) alcoholic home of two using addicts. From age 0-5, I accompanied them to all of their drunken parties and all of their daily happy hours. Those earliest years were filled with the normal consequences of being a baby to addicted parents: I WAS LOST IN THE CONFUSION OF THEIR ADDICTION.

I remember the exhilarating excitement/thrill/recklessness of riding in the baby seat of my mom's bike. I remember the absence of my parents many afternoons as they drank inside a neighbor's house as I played in the backyard entertaining myself alone. I remember many occasions waiting fully dressed in outdoor winter gear to go on a promised adventure only to wake up sweaty and still waiting and usually not going.

I remember being unattended in the car for long periods of time and once finally deciding to try driving myself (my parents watched in horror from inside as their baby moved the shifter and the car rolled out of the driveway into the street). I remember the night at one of the parties when an older son taking care of a 3-year-old me in the next room sexually molested me. And I remember the culminating drunken fight that included my gun-yielding grandfather forbidding my father from driving me while drunk 3 hours back home.

That fateful night forever changed my life!

My days of being physically lost in the confusion of using addicts were over!

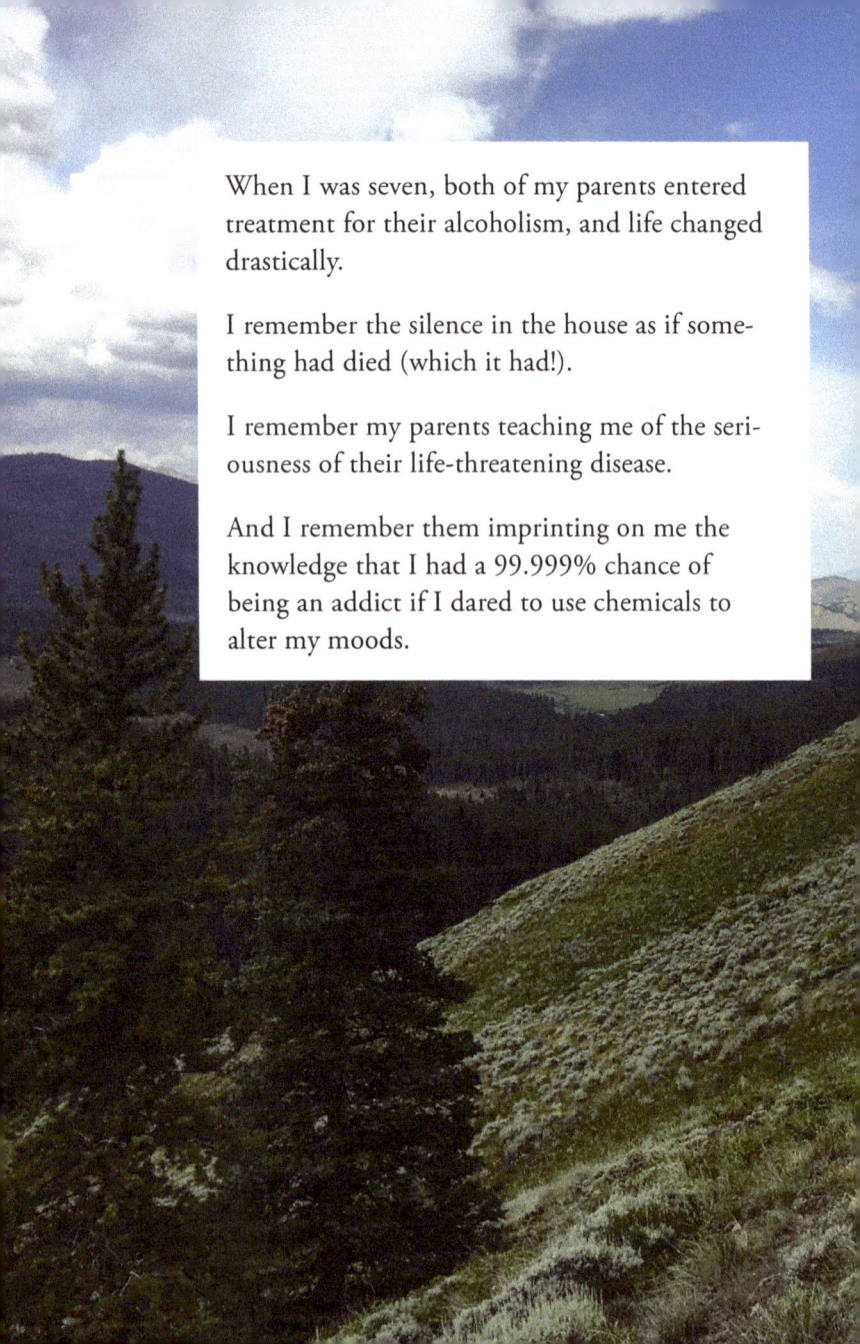

When I was seven, both of my parents entered treatment for their alcoholism, and life changed drastically.

I remember the silence in the house as if something had died (which it had!).

I remember my parents teaching me of the seriousness of their life-threatening disease.

And I remember them imprinting on me the knowledge that I had a 99.999% chance of being an addict if I dared to use chemicals to alter my moods.

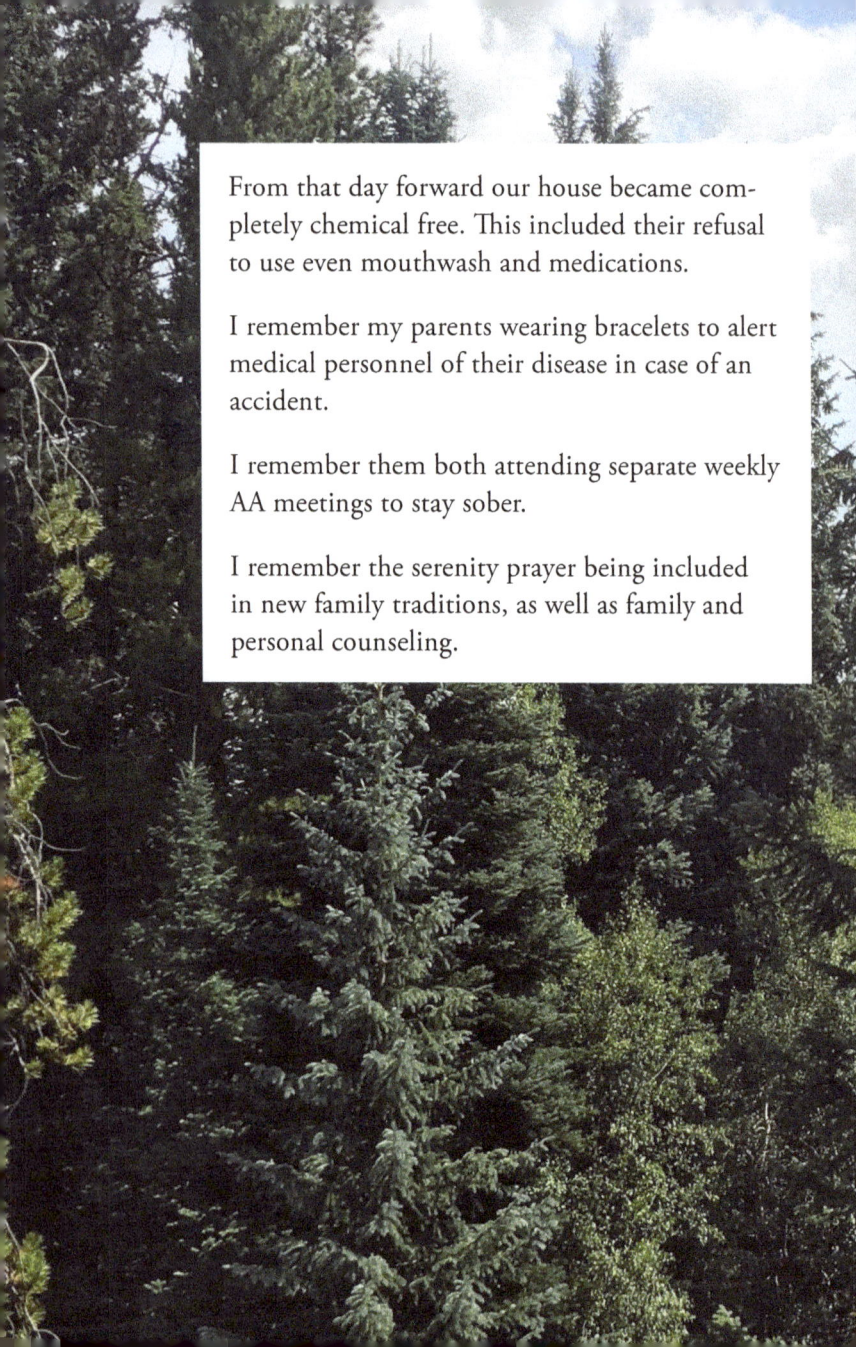

From that day forward our house became completely chemical free. This included their refusal to use even mouthwash and medications.

I remember my parents wearing bracelets to alert medical personnel of their disease in case of an accident.

I remember them both attending separate weekly AA meetings to stay sober.

I remember the serenity prayer being included in new family traditions, as well as family and personal counseling.

These early life experiences made me feel like a hybrid.

Half of me came to accept the life-threatening disease of alcoholism and the necessity of lifelong sobriety.

The other half of me included the feelings of confusion, loss and coming in second to (other) alcoholics.

This is also how I spent many years as a young adult and adult.

Part Two
Jane

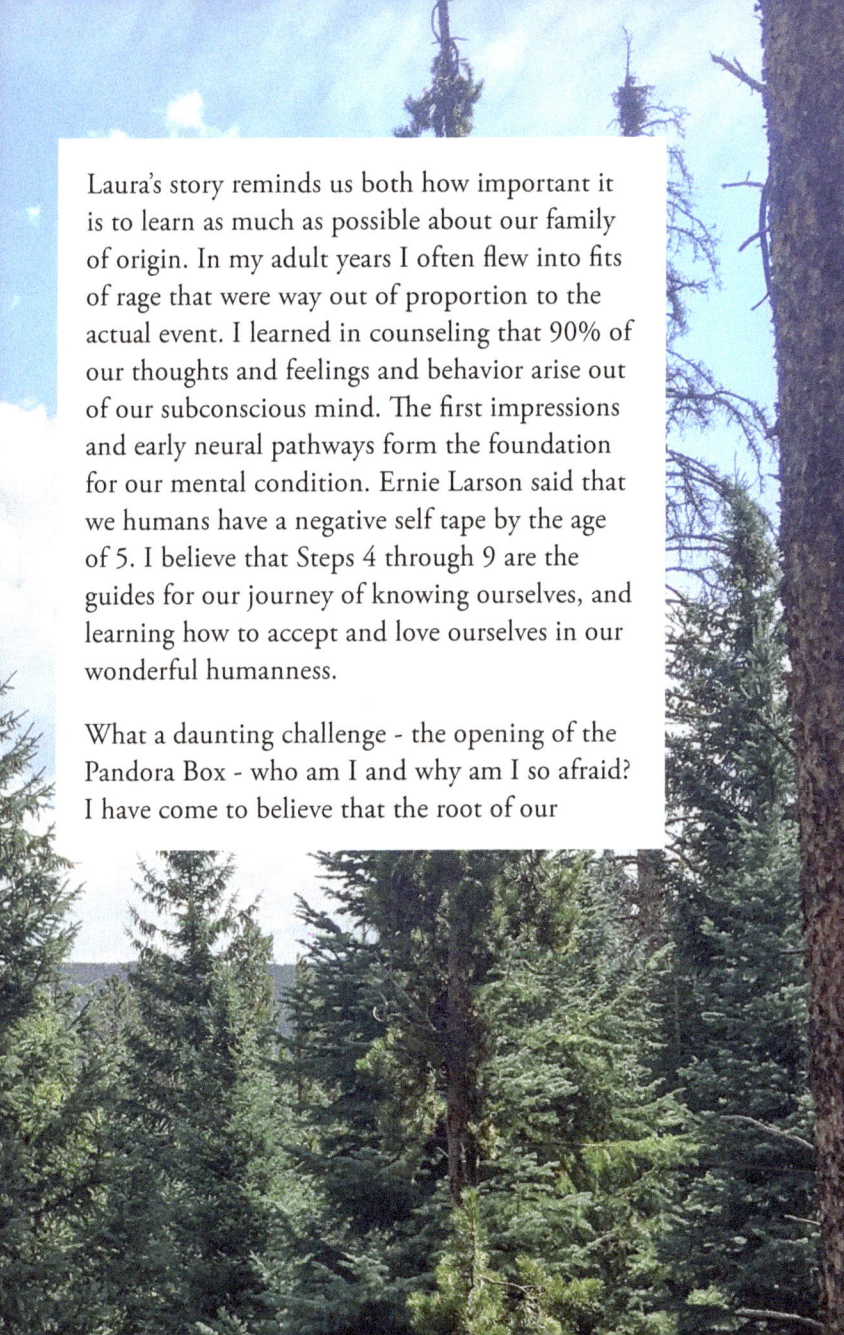

Laura's story reminds us both how important it is to learn as much as possible about our family of origin. In my adult years I often flew into fits of rage that were way out of proportion to the actual event. I learned in counseling that 90% of our thoughts and feelings and behavior arise out of our subconscious mind. The first impressions and early neural pathways form the foundation for our mental condition. Ernie Larson said that we humans have a negative self tape by the age of 5. I believe that Steps 4 through 9 are the guides for our journey of knowing ourselves, and learning how to accept and love ourselves in our wonderful humanness.

What a daunting challenge - the opening of the Pandora Box - who am I and why am I so afraid? I have come to believe that the root of our

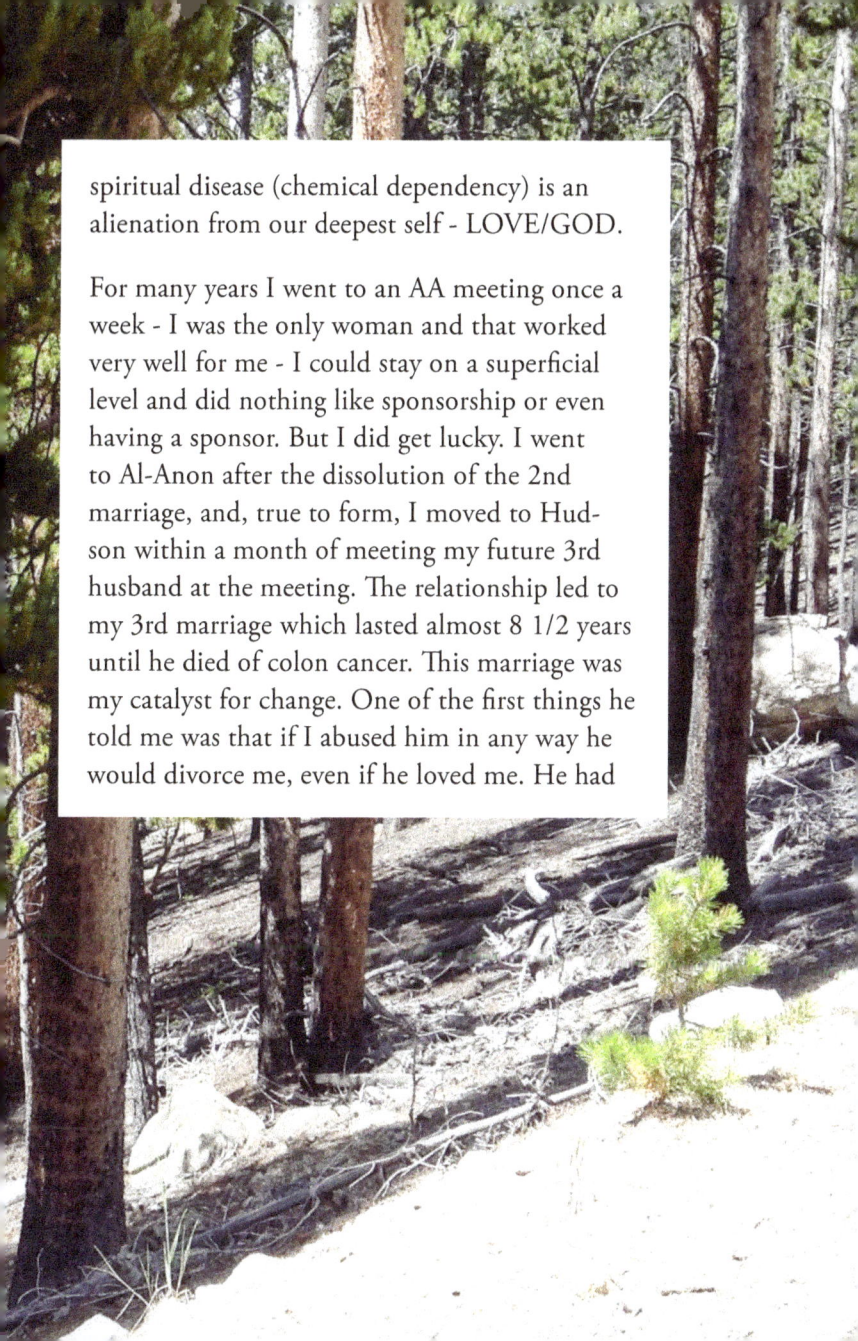

spiritual disease (chemical dependency) is an alienation from our deepest self - LOVE/GOD.

For many years I went to an AA meeting once a week - I was the only woman and that worked very well for me - I could stay on a superficial level and did nothing like sponsorship or even having a sponsor. But I did get lucky. I went to Al-Anon after the dissolution of the 2nd marriage, and, true to form, I moved to Hudson within a month of meeting my future 3rd husband at the meeting. The relationship led to my 3rd marriage which lasted almost 8 1/2 years until he died of colon cancer. This marriage was my catalyst for change. One of the first things he told me was that if I abused him in any way he would divorce me, even if he loved me. He had

worked too hard to gain his self-respect and would not jeopardize one iota of that gift. On one of our first dates he really shut me up by informing me that I sounded like a nun when I was eloquently describing that Sunday's homily on the Trinity in my effort to re-Catholicize him. That was my last Mass for many years. He visited my family with me and on the trip home completely overwhelmed me by honestly stating that he did not know how I had survived the brutality heaped upon me by my parents and siblings. It seemed to him that I was the scapegoat for all that ailed them. He was sure right.

The time had come for me to pay attention to my "Gestalt formations" - the earliest unconsious tapes of my negative addictive thoughts. Before I was born my dad supported the wives and children of his three brothers serving in the war.

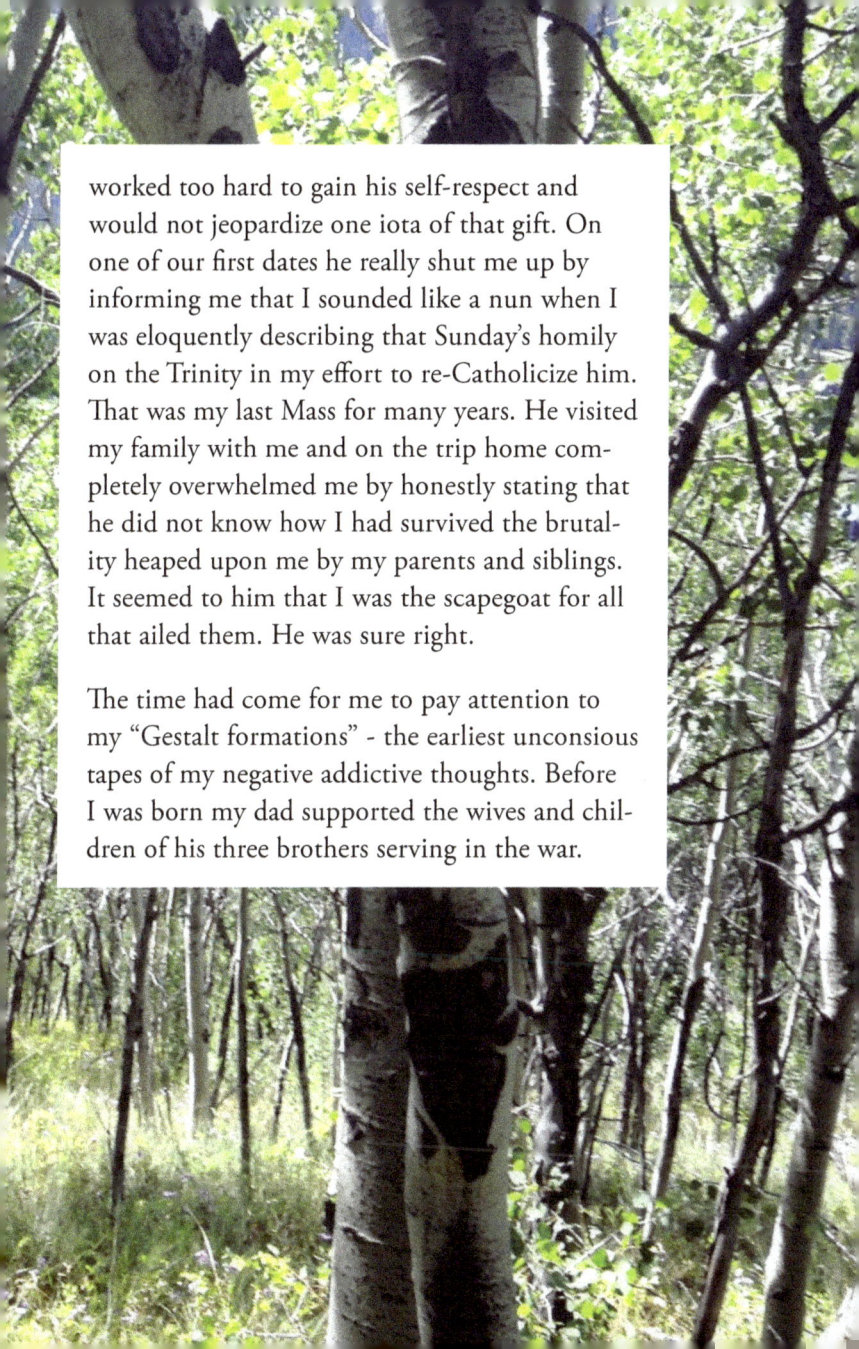

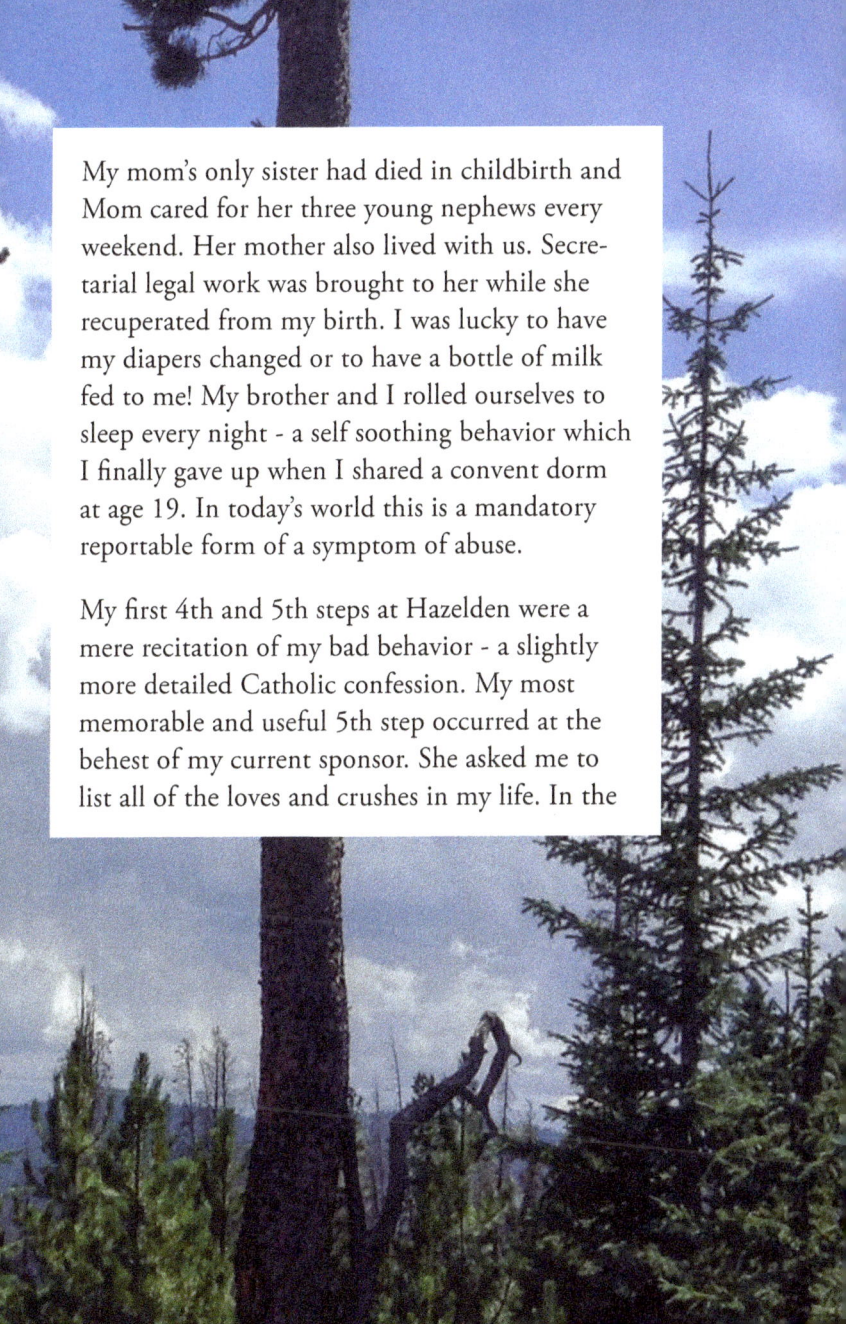

My mom's only sister had died in childbirth and Mom cared for her three young nephews every weekend. Her mother also lived with us. Secretarial legal work was brought to her while she recuperated from my birth. I was lucky to have my diapers changed or to have a bottle of milk fed to me! My brother and I rolled ourselves to sleep every night - a self soothing behavior which I finally gave up when I shared a convent dorm at age 19. In today's world this is a mandatory reportable form of a symptom of abuse.

My first 4th and 5th steps at Hazelden were a mere recitation of my bad behavior - a slightly more detailed Catholic confession. My most memorable and useful 5th step occurred at the behest of my current sponsor. She asked me to list all of the loves and crushes in my life. In the

subsequent 9th step of writing letters of amends which were torn up by me I also tore up and threw away the shards of deep shame and guilt. I recognized the repetitive theme - I saw my loneliness, my need for acceptance and affection/love, and the hole I was trying to fill in all the wrong places. When my third husband was dying, he suggested that I might be lonely and that I might consider going to AA again - for the past couple of years I had gone only to an occasional Al-Anon meeting. I told him I would get a puppy instead and I did. It worked for six months and then I found myself at a Saturday morning AA meeting and, much to my surprise, my tears flowed because I felt I had come home after a very long journey. That was in 2003. Later that year we formed a women's group and, for the first time in my life, I found women that I grew

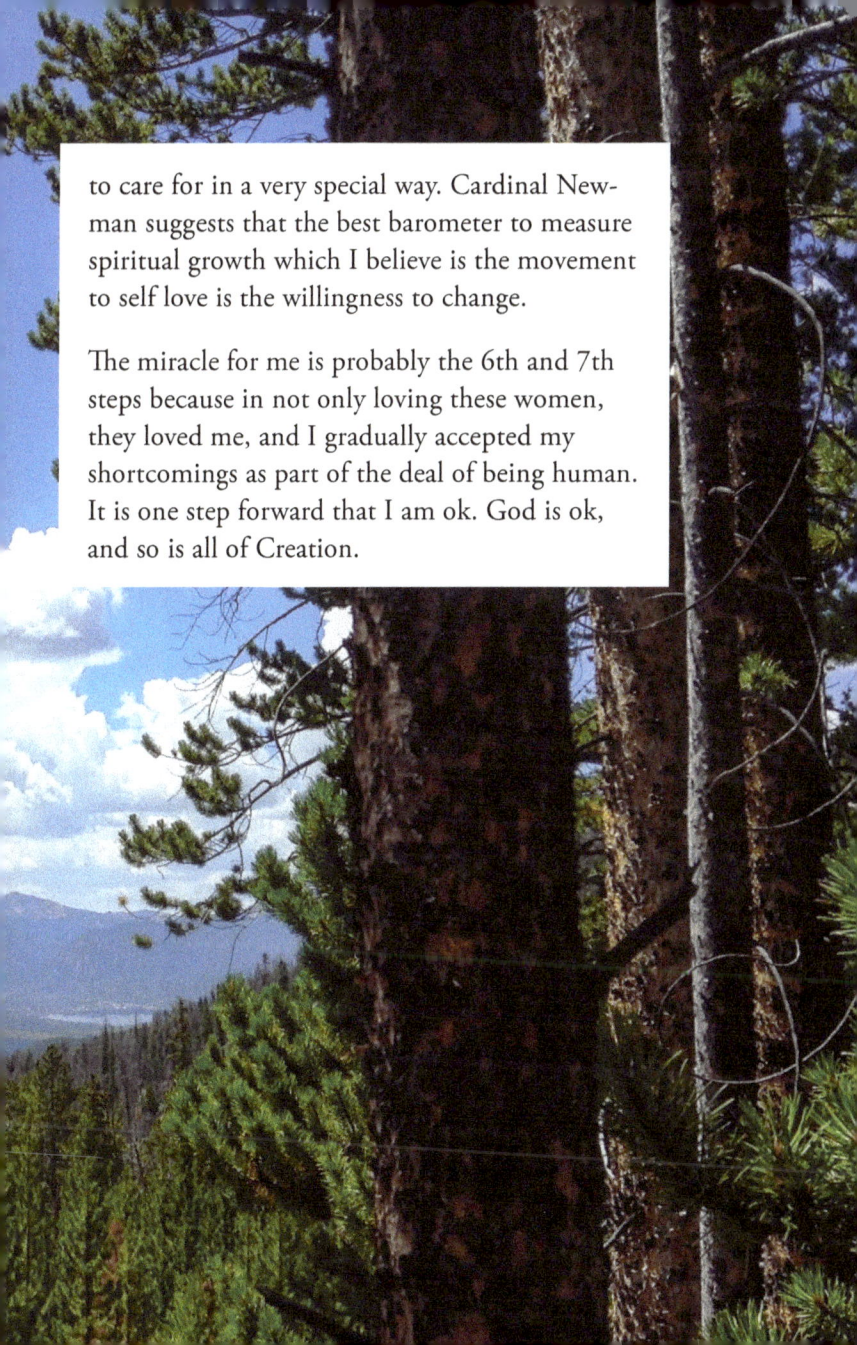

to care for in a very special way. Cardinal Newman suggests that the best barometer to measure spiritual growth which I believe is the movement to self love is the willingness to change.

The miracle for me is probably the 6th and 7th steps because in not only loving these women, they loved me, and I gradually accepted my shortcomings as part of the deal of being human. It is one step forward that I am ok. God is ok, and so is all of Creation.

Part Two
Laura

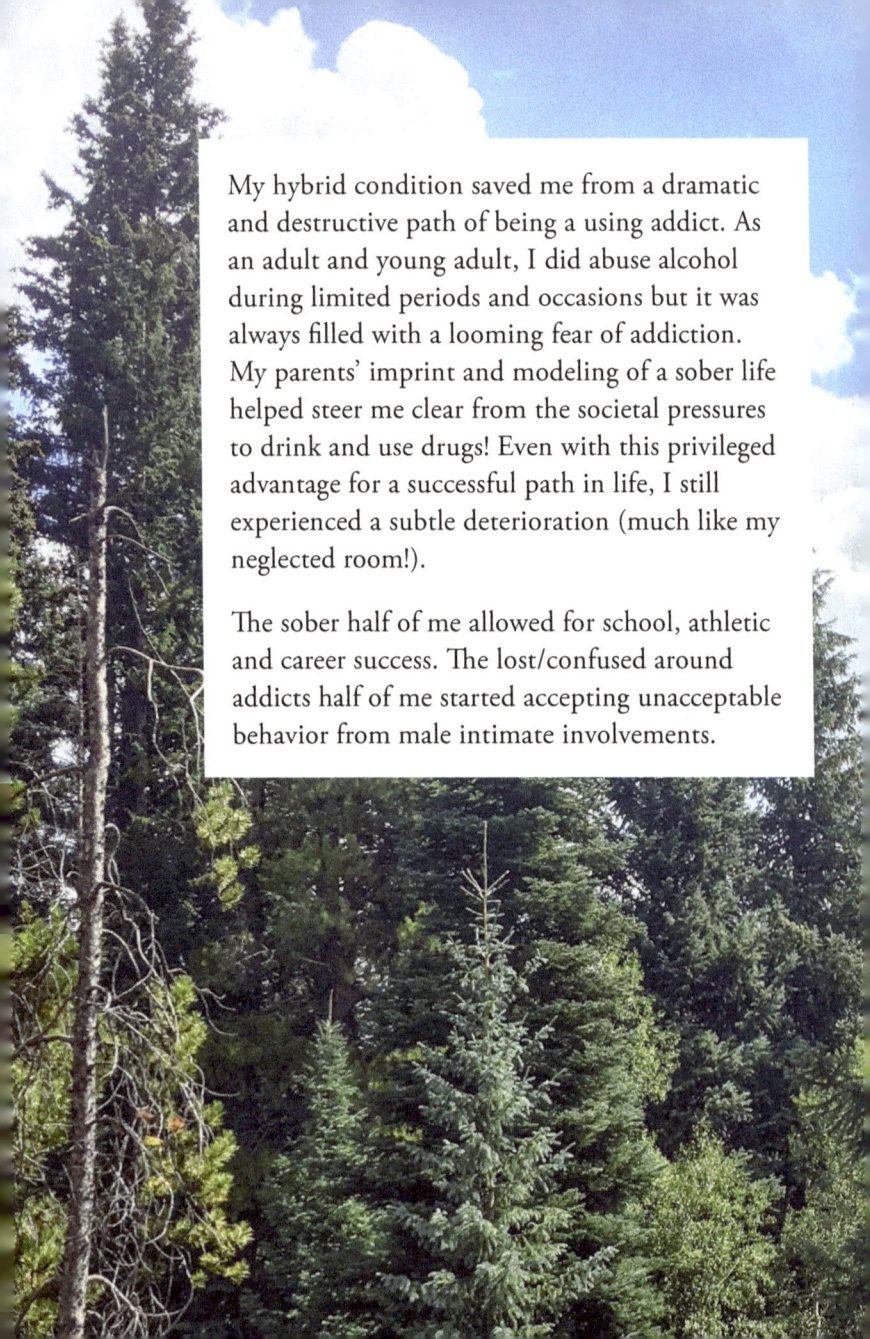

My hybrid condition saved me from a dramatic and destructive path of being a using addict. As an adult and young adult, I did abuse alcohol during limited periods and occasions but it was always filled with a looming fear of addiction. My parents' imprint and modeling of a sober life helped steer me clear from the societal pressures to drink and use drugs! Even with this privileged advantage for a successful path in life, I still experienced a subtle deterioration (much like my neglected room!).

The sober half of me allowed for school, athletic and career success. The lost/confused around addicts half of me started accepting unacceptable behavior from male intimate involvements.

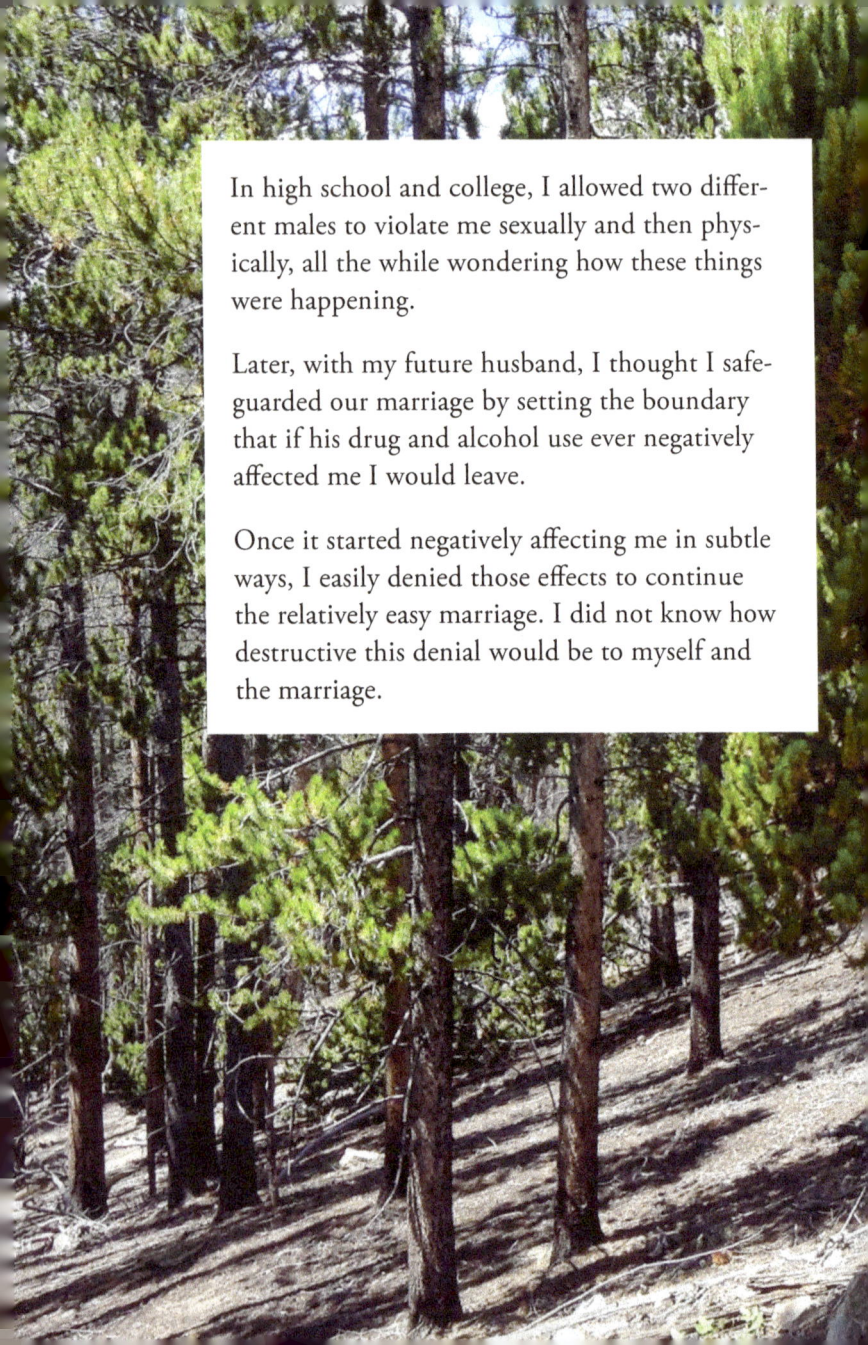

In high school and college, I allowed two different males to violate me sexually and then physically, all the while wondering how these things were happening.

Later, with my future husband, I thought I safeguarded our marriage by setting the boundary that if his drug and alcohol use ever negatively affected me I would leave.

Once it started negatively affecting me in subtle ways, I easily denied those effects to continue the relatively easy marriage. I did not know how destructive this denial would be to myself and the marriage.

Again, I accepted unacceptable behaviors and lived many years in fear of how his excessive use if found out could ruin my career. He always acted loving/polite/respectful and careful not to let his use abuse me directly in any way.

As time passed, the stress of his life was indirectly affecting my peace of mind, space and well-being.

When after 15 years the marriage finally collapsed, I again safeguarded myself by leaving what felt like a sinking ship.

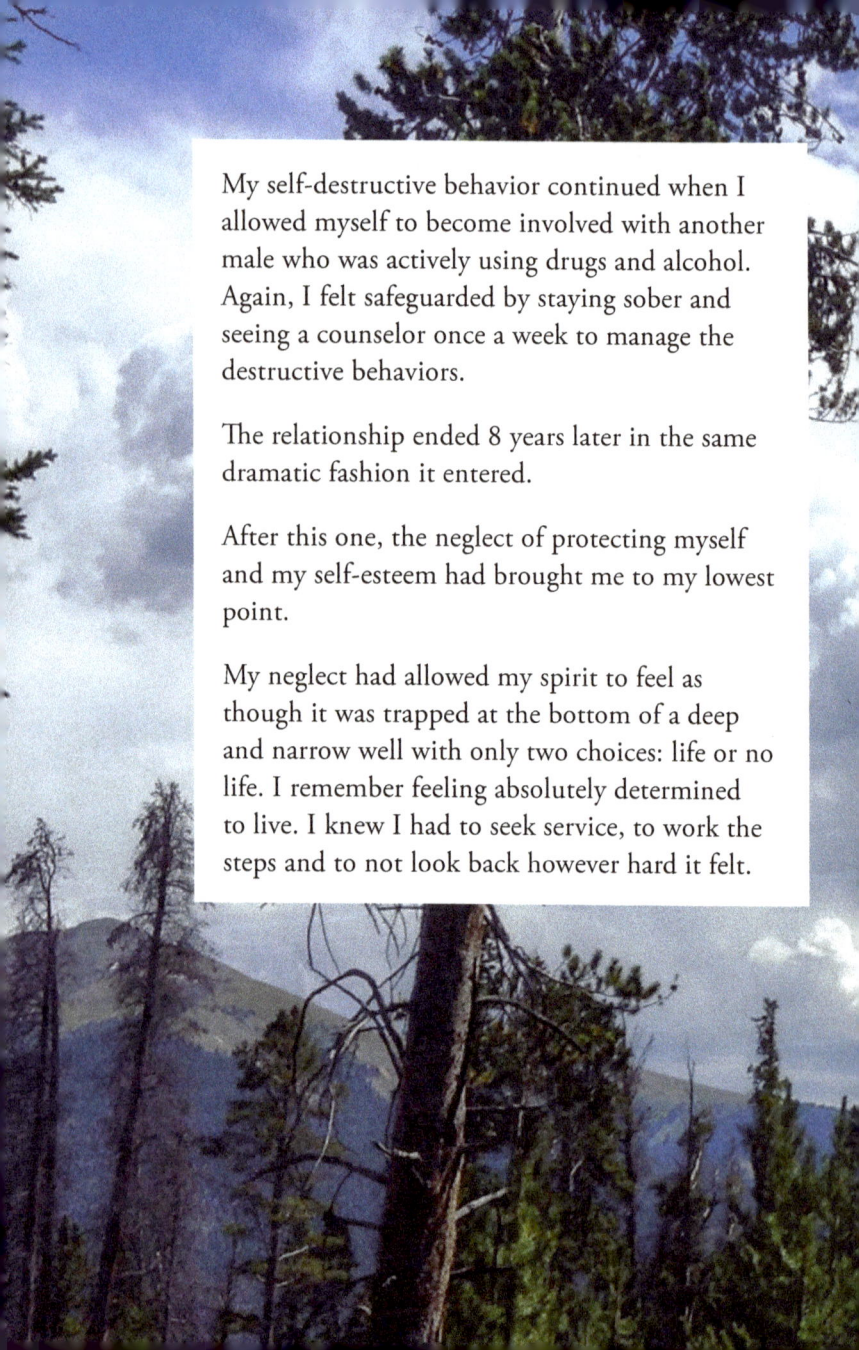

My self-destructive behavior continued when I allowed myself to become involved with another male who was actively using drugs and alcohol. Again, I felt safeguarded by staying sober and seeing a counselor once a week to manage the destructive behaviors.

The relationship ended 8 years later in the same dramatic fashion it entered.

After this one, the neglect of protecting myself and my self-esteem had brought me to my lowest point.

My neglect had allowed my spirit to feel as though it was trapped at the bottom of a deep and narrow well with only two choices: life or no life. I remember feeling absolutely determined to live. I knew I had to seek service, to work the steps and to not look back however hard it felt.

I struggled second by second for many, many months.

I clutched Hazelden's *Acceptance* pamphlet and added quotes to every page. The pages are almost disintegrated from carrying it and turning to it many times throughout the days.

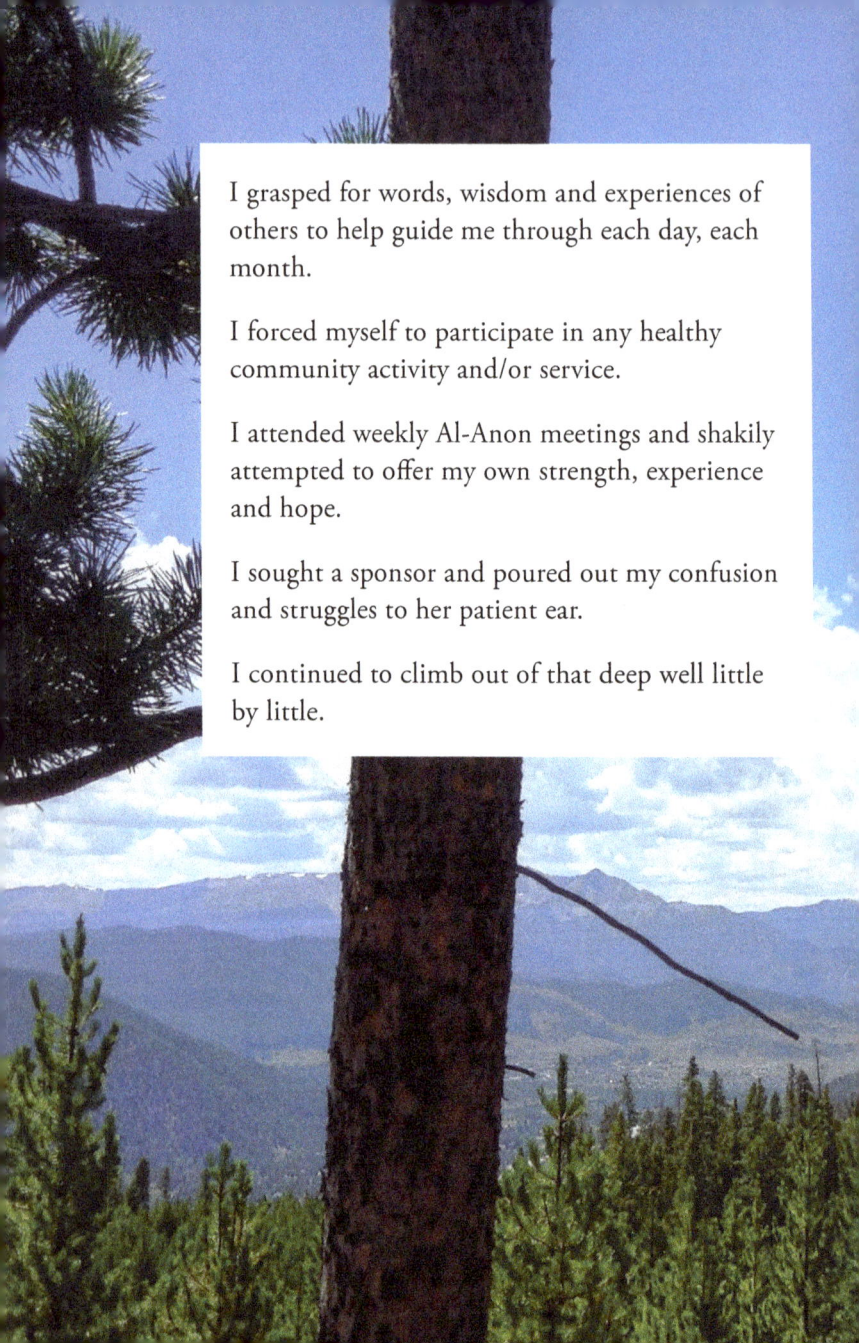

I grasped for words, wisdom and experiences of others to help guide me through each day, each month.

I forced myself to participate in any healthy community activity and/or service.

I attended weekly Al-Anon meetings and shakily attempted to offer my own strength, experience and hope.

I sought a sponsor and poured out my confusion and struggles to her patient ear.

I continued to climb out of that deep well little by little.

Part Three
Jane

My favorite teacher, Richard Rohr, says that 98% of people are like electric wires and, if the voltage and current are unsafe and unusable, the wire continues to conduct unsafe and unusable voltage and current. On some electric poles are big gray boxes that are called transformers. Their job is to make that unsafe and unusable voltage and current safe and usable. Hurt people hurt people. 98% of people pass on the hatred, the abuse, the name calling.

We in Alcoholics Anonymous have the tools to become transformers - we learn to hold the suffering/pain by naming it and taking responsibility for it and finally surrendering and accepting it. Then we can re-communicate that negative energy into a positive force.

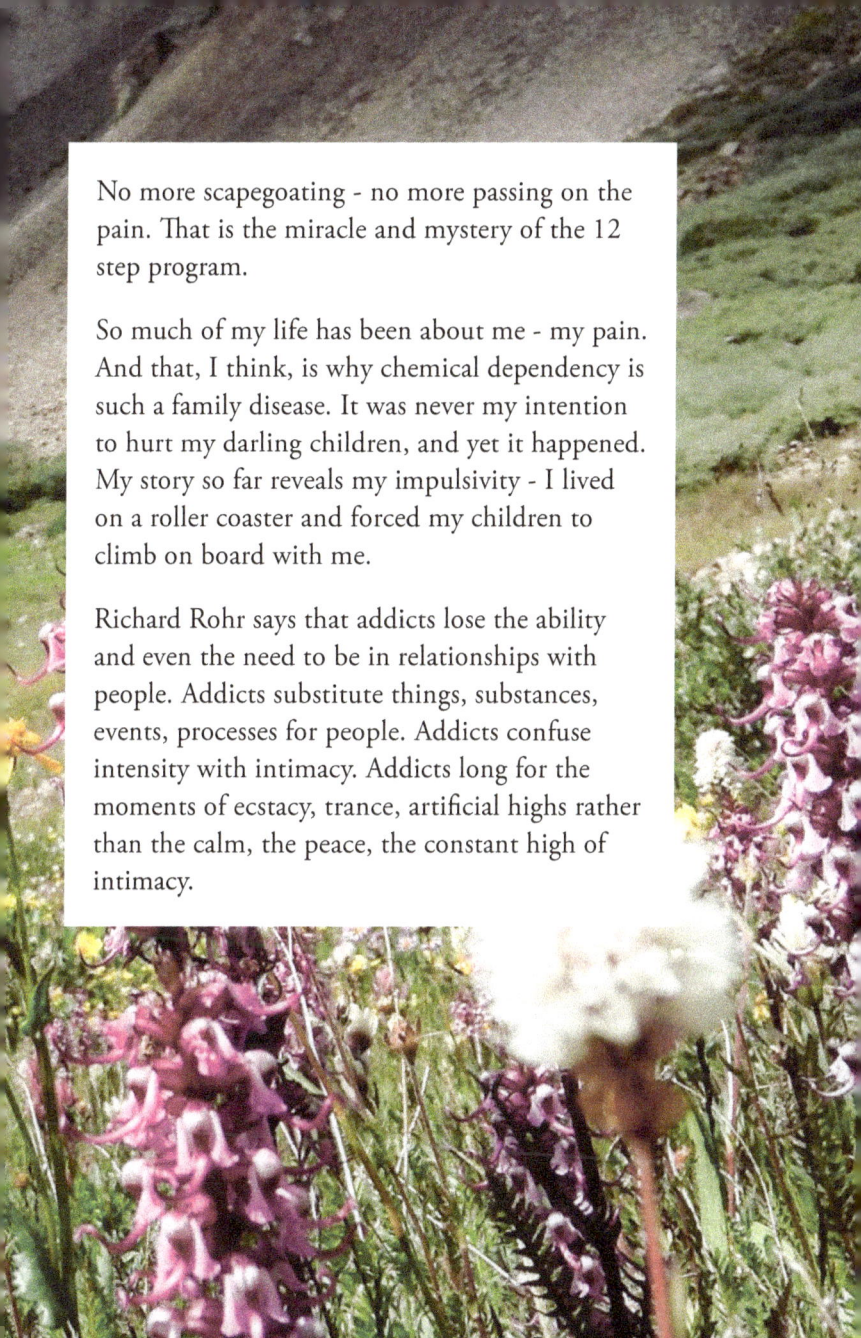

No more scapegoating - no more passing on the pain. That is the miracle and mystery of the 12 step program.

So much of my life has been about me - my pain. And that, I think, is why chemical dependency is such a family disease. It was never my intention to hurt my darling children, and yet it happened. My story so far reveals my impulsivity - I lived on a roller coaster and forced my children to climb on board with me.

Richard Rohr says that addicts lose the ability and even the need to be in relationships with people. Addicts substitute things, substances, events, processes for people. Addicts confuse intensity with intimacy. Addicts long for the moments of ecstacy, trance, artificial highs rather than the calm, the peace, the constant high of intimacy.

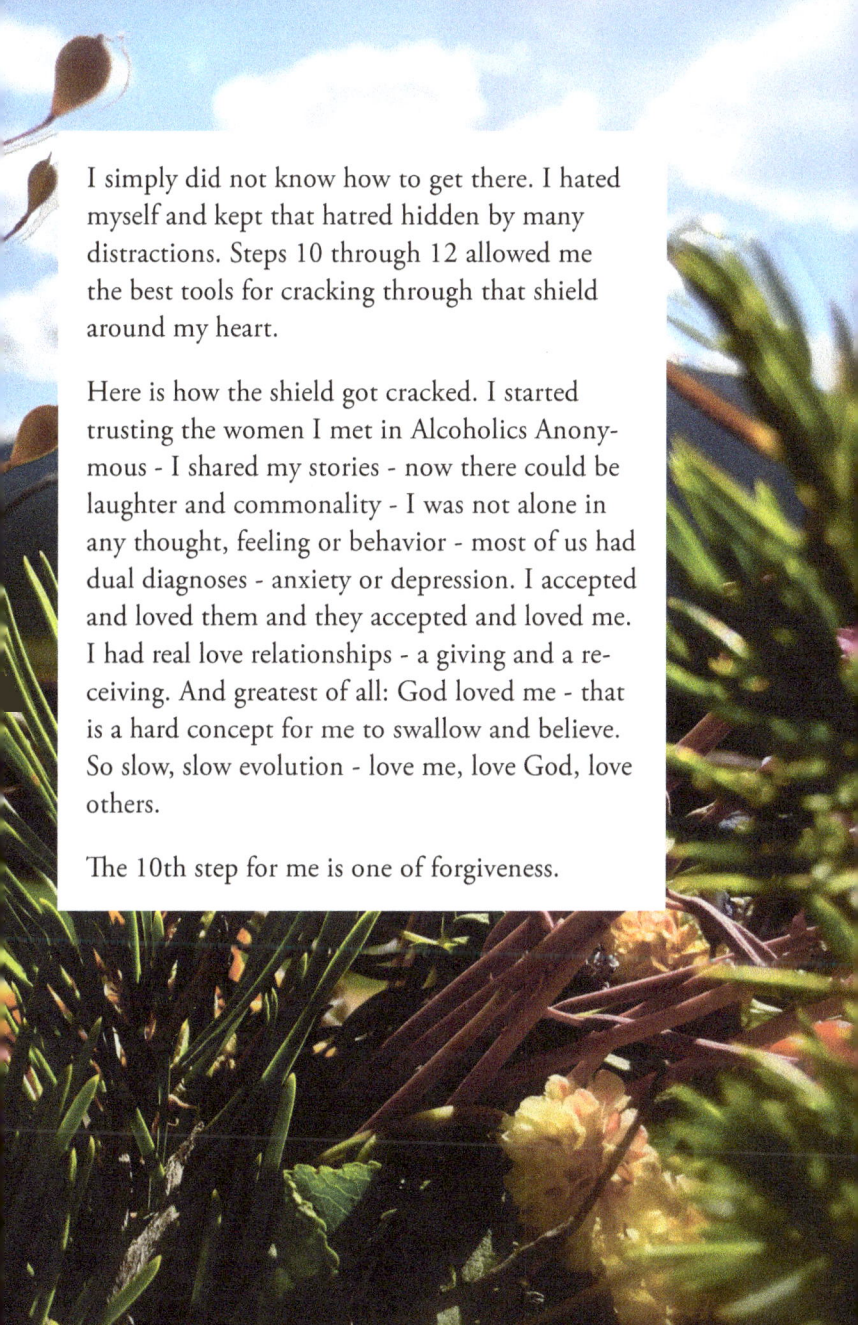

I simply did not know how to get there. I hated myself and kept that hatred hidden by many distractions. Steps 10 through 12 allowed me the best tools for cracking through that shield around my heart.

Here is how the shield got cracked. I started trusting the women I met in Alcoholics Anonymous - I shared my stories - now there could be laughter and commonality - I was not alone in any thought, feeling or behavior - most of us had dual diagnoses - anxiety or depression. I accepted and loved them and they accepted and loved me. I had real love relationships - a giving and a receiving. And greatest of all: God loved me - that is a hard concept for me to swallow and believe. So slow, slow evolution - love me, love God, love others.

The 10th step for me is one of forgiveness.

I screw up. Oh well - I apologize and move on to the next mistake. Let it go! I am human. Gratitude is the attitude - even mistakes because I can learn from them. And it is so wonderful to accept our human condition. And God cannot love any one of us less because that would not be Infinite Love. I had to learn it is only necessary for me to forgive myself and to dive into that River of Grace - always there to be received by the Perfect Giver. I truly believe in the power of meditation. It is enlightening to observe this organ, called the brain, and simply be aware of the flow of thoughts and feelings and to notice how the brain just keeps repeating the same old addictive thoughts. I have been told that in meditation it is possible to go to a deeper place of no thoughts. Perhaps it will happen for me. I am uncomfortable sitting still and lack the desire to do so. I do walk a couple hours each day and I

do my walking surrounded by beauty. I hope that counts a little for quieting my mind. God does not seem to give me hints of what God's will for me actually is but life just keeps happening to me. The best I can do is to go along with whatever happens: losing a sailboat race or getting a quadruple bogie or getting a flat tire. Whatever - all is good if I have faith and not fear.

Step 12 tells me to treat everything with respect. If it is created, it is good because it has been in the Mind of God from before time. I tend to ignore the hierarchies of government, commerce, religion and trust that it will all turn out ok. There is joy in the ordinary. There is no boredom. There is no loneliness. The hole in my soul is filled with the deepest me/God. And as I become older, I am no longer filled with fear as filled with the childlike faith that life is fun

and filled with butterflies and puppy dogs. I will close with a few lines from my favorite mystic, Thomas Mertin: "It is necessary for me to see the first point of light that begins to be dawn It is necessary to be alone at the resurrection of Day in solemn silence at which the sun appears, for at this moment all the affairs of cities, of governments, of war departments, are seen to be the bickering of mice. I receive from the Eastern woods, the tall oaks, the one word DAY. It is never the same. It is always in a totally new language."

Part Three
Laura

The past two years of working the steps of Al-Anon, dedicated attendance of meetings, finding and utilizing a sponsor, repeatedly reading and rereading slogans and literature saved my spirit and saved me.

Without the 4th step,

...without the patience and love of my sponsor,

...without the loving exchanges and interactions and encouragement and acceptance of the fellowship,

...without the constant reminders of *Just for Today*,

...without acceptance,

...without daily inventories,

...without the 10th step and then promptly admitting wrongs,

...without turning my life over to a higher power,

...without prayer,

...without meditation,

...without service,

...without service,

...without service, my life would be without hope, without possibilities, without me.

Today my life is very different!

I diligently work the program of Al-Anon.

I diligently attend a weekly meeting.

I diligently read Al-Anon literature.

I diligently participate in sponsorship.

I diligently do something every day I don't want to do.

I diligently find ways to serve the fellowship, students and the community.

I know now and have the tools to take 100%, full responsibility for my well-being, my life and my happiness.

I am no longer a hybrid!

Daily diligence working the program, being involved in the fellowship and the greater community and turning life over to a higher power has made me feel whole/complete/myself.

I am a grateful spirit continually healing on and contributing to the road to recovery.

ALL PROCEEDS FROM THE SALE OF THIS BOOK GO TO THE

HAZELDEN BETTY FORD FOUNDATION

www.ingramcontent.com/pod-product-compliance
Lightning Source LLC
Chambersburg PA
CBHW040329300426
44113CB00020B/2704